MW00676439
Dear
Suzanne
Wishing you all the
Best.
Hare Krishna
Krishna Priya Dasi
2017

Endorsements

"As the lotus flowers unfold, revealing their depth of beauty, so the verses in this little book, entitled *Lotus Lyrics*, unfold, revealing expressions of devotional wisdom. These expressions of a true devotee of the divinity of Krishna are presented with an endearing simplicity that reaches out to the reader's heart. Many of the complex ideas of the *Bhagavad-gita As It Is*, authored and translated by A.C. Bhaktivedanta Swami Prabhupada, are made easily accessible and sweetly comprehensible in these delightful lyrical verses."

– Graham M. Schweig, Ph.D.,
Associate Professor of Religion, Director of the Indic Studies Program, Christopher Newport University, Author and translator of *Dance of Divine Love* and *Bhagavad Gita: The Beloved Lord's Secret Love Song*

Lotus Lyrics, Second Edition, is Krishna Priya's fourth published book of poems. In it she systematically elaborates on some key themes of transcendental thought and, in a sutra form, analyzes profound philosophical truths revealing the nature of the self and the Divine, and the relationship between both. As seen in the titles of her poems, she has succeeded in delineating the multivariate approaches to the mystical realm. Yet, in a very clear and realized manner she shares her insights at a level that all can understand. I recommend this book of poems to the sincere theo-philosopher and to all seekers of the truth..

– Lucrecia U. Maclachlan, Meredith College, Raleigh, NC

"I have known Krishna Priya Dasi for more than 20 years (in India) when her parents approached me to teach her English. She used to ask for my help converting her Hindi poems into English. I realized, even from the beginning, that she was an extra-intelligent student. Her poetry book, *Lotus Lyrics*, touched me very deeply and I am very proud of her."

– Hari Narayan Mathur, English teacher

I was the one who diagnosed Krishna Priya Dasi's major problem in her brain. She was operated on in Mumbai. After surgery, she was under my care and treatment. Her will power, positive nature and faith to her Lord Krishna and her spiritual master were amazing. I am completely thrilled to read her poetry book, *Lotus Lyrics* written even while she was facing severe health challenges. Her poems will elevate her to a higher stage so she can be an inspiration to others who have severe health challenges. My patients will definitely get strength by her enlivening efforts.

– Dr.Anjani Kumar Sharma, MD, DM Neurology [AIMS, Delhi], Consultant Neurologist, Assoc.Professor Neurology

"This simple and uplifting poetry offering invites us into the gentle heart of the author and simultaneously beckons our own inner awakening. It was written at a time of personal distress, but the mood is one of faith, prayer, and wisdom. Like the lotus flowers that adorn it, which simultaneously live in the water and rise above it, the author and her poetry appear to be of this world, but do not, in actuality touch it. A pure and inspired work eloquently presented in English by a saintly lady for whom the English language is not her native tongue.

– Karen E. Silberstein ND, PhD, Conscious Being Wellness Services

"Krishna Priya's poetry is an inspiration to read. The poetry is beautiful and descriptive, and as a dance teacher and choreographer it is a wonderful medium to interpret. Her work is from the soul. It is always a great pleasure for me to dance based on her poems at my programs."

– Gaurangi-priya Gopal, artistic director, Prema Natya Vidyalaya Dance School

His Divine Grace
A.C. Bhaktivedanta Swami Prabhupada
The Author of *Bhagavad-gita As It Is*

The lotus blooms in water and being untouched
Gives its beauty, color, inspiration and fragrance.
The pure devotee in this world is not affected by it
And spreads Krishna consciousness by his presence.

The lotus-eyed Divine Couple, Sri Radha and Krishna
Perform Their divine pastimes on a lotus seat.
Their special mercy is like the lotus flower
Cooling, aromatic, beautiful and sweet.

Lotus Lyrics

SECOND EDITION

Krishna Priya Dasi

Art by Krishna Priya Dasi

For more information please contact the author at
krsnapriyad@hotmail.com

Edited by Jnanagamya Das, Nancie Rosenberg, and
MadanMohanMohini Dasi

This Edition design and layout by Mayapriya Dasi, Bookwrights

First Edition design and layout by Kurma Rupa Dasa

Printed in China by Palace Press International

Second Edition

ISBN 978-0-9797406-0-2

Dedication

Dedicated to all special souls
Who deliver the message of God
For unity, peace, love and laughter
In an inspiring, illuminating mode.

They never lose hope or harmony
Even facing heavy physical challenges.
Their deep determination and devotion
Will bring to the world wondrous changes.

Contents

Preface

Dear Friends,

My special thanks to my known and unknown friends for their encouragement and appreciation for the first edition of my poetry book, 'Lotus Lyrics'. Your inspiring words have brightened my way to try to do something that may be helpful to others.

It is a great feeling to share the experiences of my life with all of you. I was born in Rajasthan, India with heavy physical challenges. Though I was loved and cared for by my family, still my mind was not happy and peaceful due to my disability. The bodily conception and the desire to live a normal life were very deep in my consciousness.

Sometimes in life something special suddenly happens where life starts to flow in an enlivening direction. It happened in my life when my father gave me one book called 'Bhagavad-gita As It Is' by His Divine Grace A.C. Bhaktivedanta Swami Prabhupada. The study of this transcendental literature brightened my dark thinking and introduced me to illuminating teachings. I understood that we are not this temporary body but are the eternal spirit soul, part and parcel of the Supreme Spirit Lord Krishna. "Those who are wise lament neither for the living nor for the dead". Bg 2.11 These words inspired me to no longer lament for my bodily situation, but to begin to develop my love for God. Once the love of God develops, one starts to see all living entities with equal vision, treating them as the parts of the Supreme Personality of Godhead, Lord Krishna, with all love, care and respect.

The divine messages of the *Bhagavad-gita As It Is* encouraged me to write poems on these transcendental teachings and share them with others. But at that time, I did not work on them. In April, 2005, I faced another heavy challenge, as I had to undergo major brain surgery. I had a complicated and uncommon brain disease; my brain was dislocated and had slipped down towards my spinal cord. In most cases, the result of this disease meant either death or a life worse than death. I struggled between life and death for a very long period of time. At that critical time, my biggest pain was that I did not write the poems that were in my heart.

Prayers possess priceless power that can change anyone's destiny. I give credit for their sincere prayers to my spiritual master, devotees, family, friends, doctors, nurses, and above all, for the special mercy of the Supreme Personality of Godhead, Lord Krishna, for saving my life in a miraculous way. I had to stay in a completely dark and lonely room for a long time because even a little bit of light and sound were extremely painful for my brain and eyes. There was also a chance of getting a brain infection. Who was my companion in that lonely and desolate room? One verse from Bhagavad-gita As It Is kept running through my consciousness. It is from the 2nd chapter, text 14, where Lord Krishna tells His intimate friend and devotee Arjuna:

"O son of Kunti, the nonpermanent appearance of happiness and distress, and their disappearance in due course, are like appearance and disappearance of winter and summer seasons. They arise from sense perception, O scion of Bharata, and one must learn to tolerate them without being disturbed."

By repeating this verse over and over in my mind, I got the overwhelming feeling that one day this situation would be over and I would be able to see the beautiful form of my lotus-eyed Lord Krishna and would be able to listen to songs of God. It happened so smoothly, and gave me such positive energy, that this verse brought me out of what appeared to be a very dark and doomed situation.

At the end of 2006, I stayed in Vrindavan, the sacred land of Lord Krishna, where I wrote most of the poems in this book. I also did some simple lotus paintings there, although I had to change my traditional style. I did not want to miss my second and rare chance, even though I was experiencing severe dizziness and non-coordination between my eyes, hand and brain.

I tried to write the deep and profound philosophy of *Bhagavad-gita As It Is* in simple language, though I am not sure how much success I achieved. But I humbly request everyone to make *Bhagavad-gita As It Is* a ship on the ocean of your life to help you overcome all obstacles and reach the definite destination of all bliss, knowledge and eternity. As a final note, I did not mention Lord Krishna's name directly in my poems because it does not matter what nationality or belief one adheres to. Lord Krishna's messages and teachings are perfect, profound, practical and priceless for everyone. Bhagavad-gita As It Is can be purchased at www.krishna.com.

Thank you very much. HARE KRISHNA!

Your servant and friend,

Krishna Priya Dasi

Krishna Priya Dasi

Lotus Lyrics

SECOND EDITION

The Essence

The Supreme Lord

The position of the Supreme Lord is
The supreme consciousness beyond contamination.
He is both the creator and the enjoyer
And controller of the cosmic manifestation.

The Living Entity

The position of the living entity is
Part and parcel of the Supreme Personality.
He is the person created and enjoyed
And controlled by the highest authority.

Nature

The manifestation of nature
Is not false but temporary.
The nature cycle works eternally
Though it comes and goes momentarily.

Time

Time never stays for anyone
No power can stop or hold,
It passes like a blowing wind
Not possible to be controlled.

Activity

The result of activity is certain
Whether we get it today or tomorrow.
Depending upon our different deeds,
We achieve either happiness or sorrow.

The Power of Divine Shelter

The shelter of the spiritual master
Is the essence of eternal advancement.
A serving attitude toward the learned one
Bestows genuine and fruitful achievement.

Mental speculation or dry argument
Distract one from the proven path.
Full surrender to a self-realized soul
Saves one from worldly wrath.

Combinations of inquiries and submission
Deepens one's faith and progress.
The divine leader imparts knowledge
As he follows the true spiritual process.

Service, inquiries, submission, they'll all impart
Everlasting bright personal beams;
Knowledge brings proper understanding
All beings are parts of the Supreme.

The Eternal Smile

The eternal, sweet smile exists
In nature's mode of goodness.
Purity of the mind then bestows
The treasure of real happiness.

We dance in the wondrous joy
In chanting of the holy name.
The Lord's association is gained
As we reach the absolute aim.

The name is not different
From the pure Supreme One.
Lighting up the darkness–
It's like the rising of the sun.

The Purpose of the Vedas

Men of small knowledge are attracted
To the Veda's flowery words
Which recommend fruitive activities for good birth,
Power and elevation to the heavenly worlds.

Sense gratification and opulent life–
Too tempting for them to ignore.
They think that this is the whole purpose
And that there is nothing more.

They are bewildered by the attraction
Of sense enjoyment and material opulence.
Thus their resolute determination
For devotional life loses its existence.

The Vedas deal mainly with matter
And its threefold material qualities.
Rise above them and become transcendental;
Be free from all anxieties and dualities.

The water of a great reservoir
Can serve all purposes and aims.
The purpose of the Vedas can be served
By chanting the holy names.

Just Taking One Step

One step on the devotional path
Is the greatest move ever.
It takes us eventually to the goal
And secures our place forever.

Even a little association of devotees
Lights our life's impending doom.
Even a little time in their shelter
Will wipe away sadness and gloom.

Even a little love of God
Illuminates the darkest dream.
And one drop of the spiritual master's mercy
Flows freely as a soothing stream.

Even a little offering of a flower or leaf
Can please the Almighty Supreme Lord.
A prayer can begin with only one word
To experience how His mercy is poured.

The biggest fortune is hidden
Behind the smallest start.
Even a tiny spark lights one's life
Showing the greatness of His divine heart.

The Everlasting Reward

There is no impediment, loss or diminution
By taking one step in a devotional way.
And just a little advancement on this path
Can take the most dangerous type of fear away.

Even a small beginning of service
Bestows a transcendental effect.
Even if it is not finished or completed,
The result is permanent and perfect.

One percent done in God consciousness
Bears everlasting results or fruit.
In the next life, one will begin from two percent
And continue his progress to the Absolute.

However, any work begun on the material plane
Has to be one hundred percent complete for success.
But, still, the result ends with the end of this body
And there is no chance for further progress

The Impetuous Senses

The senses are so strong and impetuous
That they forcibly carry away
The mind of a man of discrimination
Who's endeavoring to control them every day.

By attachment to these senses,
Our real consciousness is enveloped.
By sensual contemplation,
The blazing fire of lust develops.

Lust is the very reason
For causing our great anger.
We fall down into darkness
Where every step is danger.

Delusion makes its way
Through anger's bleak illusion.
Bewilderment of memory arises
From the pathway of delusion.

When memory is bewildered,
Our intelligence is fooled.
Without proper intelligence,
We fall down into the material pool.

Comtemplating the Objects of the Senses

When one contemplates the sense objects,
Such attachments become strong desires.
These attachments turn into lust
Just like a burning fire.

Anger arises from lust
Producing complete delusion.
Delusion bewilders memory
Causing enormous confusion.

Once intelligence is lost
Leaving no ray of light,
One falls down into the darkness
And loses his spiritual sight.

The Result of Roaming Senses

A strong wind sweeps away
A boat without impediment.
Endless roaming senses confine
Man's intelligence in imprisonment.

Once he loses spiritual consciousness,
Sensual addictions attack with force.
He captivates himself in delusion
And remains aloof from the real source.

The Hankering for Sense Enjoyment

The hankering for sense enjoyment
Destroys one's desire for devotion.
The mind bewildered in temporary opulence
Makes one drown in the material ocean.

A poor fund of knowledge leads one
To the path of fierce destruction.
One digs himself his own grave
Being desirous for sensual attraction.

He works hard to enjoy the fleeting body
By forgetting the soul's eternal presence.
He falls down into the obscure well
Remaining in deep-rooted ignorance.

The Cause of Happiness and Distress

Nature is said to be the cause
Of material causes and effects,
Whereas the living entities are the cause
Of pains and joys due to previous acts.

There are 8,400,000 species of life
And these are creations of the material nature.
They arise from different sensual pleasures,
From the desires of these different creatures.

When they are put into different bodies,
They face different kinds of fate.
All situations are due to their bodies;
There's only enjoyment in their original state.

Their desire to lord it over the material world
Brings them to this place.
They struggle hard to enjoy their senses and bodies
But, there's no real happiness; that is the case.

The living entities are blessed or damned
According to activities and desires of the soul.
Once they're placed in particular bodies,
Material nature puts them under her control.

Hellish Gateways

Those who are envious and mischievous
Are the lowest among all men.
I cast them into the ocean of material existence
And into demoniac species of life again.

By having to take a lower birth,
They cannot approach Me.
They gradually sink further down
Into the most abominable existence that be.

The three gateways to hell
Are lust, anger and greed.
A sane man should give these up
And from degradation he'll be freed.

Love and Lust

The real meaning of true love
Is to please the senses of the Lord.
This exalted path easily breaks
The knots of the material cord.

Lust means to please our senses
And all attempts for own satisfaction.
The worldly bondage ties us firmly;
We bear the heavy load of our action.

It is not difficult to conquer lust
By the protection of the strong shield
Which is the dust of the Lord's lotus feet
Which takes us out from this dangerous field.

The transcendental path of divine love
Takes us to the realm our eternal life.
The temporary path of increasing lust
Pushes us down into a well of strife.

Our Natural Propensity

The existence of our enemies
Is nowhere but inside.
We are captivated by
Our lust, anger, greed and pride.

The victorious crown can be gained
By developing love of the Lord.
All enemies will be defeated
And peace will be the reward.

Coverings

As fire is covered by smoke,
A mirror is cloaked by dust.
An embryo within the womb;
The living entity is veiled by lust.

Pure consciousness becomes covered
By the many lusty desires.
The enemy is never satisfied
But burns like a blazing fire.

Lust builds its residence within
The senses, mind and intelligence.
It covers the real knowledge
And one falls into ignorance.

The Mind: Our Enemy or Our Friend?

One must elevate himself
With the help of one's own mind.
He should not degrade himself
By leaving his intelligence behind.

The mind can be one's best friend
If focused on the right aim.
One achieves great success
By chanting the holy name.

The mind can be an enemy as well
If not controlled in time.
The restless mind ruins one's life
When there's lack of thoughts sublime.

The master of the subdued mind
Wins the glorious crown.
He rises up in certainty
No more to again fall down.

This person meets such great joy
And gains tranquility.
His goal is now finally achieved
With good fortune and dignity.

The Flickering Mind

Intelligence loses its existence
Without connection to the Supreme.
The mind flickers in a dark forest
And peace vanishes from the scene.

Once peace leaves its place,
Troubles and miseries increase.
If the mind is not stable and calm,
All happiness and harmony cease.

Clear Perception

Once one's mind is entirely restrained
From material, mental conception,
He sees the self clearly
And experiences deep perception.

Actual freedom follows him
With boundless joy and happiness.
All miseries depart from his life
And he lives in righteousness.

His thoughts are never shaken
Even in midst of some great pain.
He never departs from the truth
Knowing there's no greater gain.

Crossing the Ocean of Duality

By using transcendental knowledge
As a boat of purity,
Even the most sinful have crossed
The ocean of dark duality.

Once the mind is fixed
On the highest, obtainable goal,
No obstacles can block
The path to the Supreme Whole.

A faithful person acts
According to God's will.
He always controls his senses
And his desires are then fulfilled.

By all his constant efforts,
No material dirt remains.
Without doubt or delay
Full perfection he attains.

Cessation of Suffering

The honey taste cannot be relished
By licking the bottle's outer surface.
No peace of mind can be achieved
By engaging in the illusory race.

The foundation of harmony abides
In God conscious, blissful life.
Simple living and high thinking
Will save us from terrible strife.

The prime purpose of human birth
Is for spiritual life to attain,
So we never need to suffer
In the birth and death cycle again.

The Higher Taste

When one is servant of his senses,
He is no longer spiritually alert.
It is important for him to quench his thirst
Running behind a mirage in the desert.

If a person can withdraw his senses
As a tortoise withdraws into his shell,
He is no longer dictated by sense enjoyment
And is fixed in perfect consciousness quite well.

The higher taste is in the service
Of the Creator and His created offspring.
So efforts to enjoy our senses are like
The bird that wants to fly without wings.

The Benefits of Devotion

Once we are fully dependent
On the good will of the Lord,
We no longer experience dualities
And the spiritual nectar's poured.

All purposes are served at once
By the water of the great ocean.
Our ability is like a small pond
Without our love and devotion.

The Eternal Achievement

One practices with patience
And is fixed in determination.
He achieves exalted consciousness
Abandoning all mental speculation.

Working hard on his way
As a full-hearted enthusiast,
Success is certain at the end;
He is certainly a great optimist.

There is no loss or delay
On the path of pure devotion.
Even a single step towards it
Saves one from the dangerous ocean.

A little advancement on the sacred path
Eventually takes one to the Supreme.
There is no trial or any pain
And rejoicing exists in the extreme.

Inspiration

Waters of the river
Flow into the sea.
The sea accepts the waves
Without changing to any degree.

The sea is filled with water
But doesn't cross its limit.
It sets a good example
For other beings to benefit.

Likewise, the waves of desire
Don't disturb a learned soul.
He achieves inner peace
And goes towards the real goal.

The Lord Carries What We Need

Devotees never fall into illusion;
The Lord carries what they need.
They worship with exclusive devotion
Planting in others' hearts the spiritual seed.

As the result of sincere service,
The Lord preserves what they possess.
Whenever challenging moments arise
The Supreme Soul is there to bless.

Achieving Transcendence

No extra efforts are required
To control our material senses.
The loving service to God
Elevates us to transcendence.

No chance along the way
For temporary, material engagements.
The pure devotional life
Blesses one with wonderful achievements.

The spiritual nectar's relished
Once the taste finally increases.
No other desire remains
And all worldly attraction ceases.

Fragrant flowers bloom
By the spiritual flowing stream.
Spring is brightly shining
With a beautiful sparkling beam.

The goal is ever nearer
With each step along the road.
Full knowledge and bliss abound
When one walks toward the eternal abode.

How to Become Satisfied

Just by pouring some water
On the roots of any tree,
The branches, twigs, roots and leaves
Grow as they should be.

Just by supplying some food
To the stomach of the living spirit,
The senses of the body
Automatically gain great benefit.

All living beings become satisfied
By pleasing the Supreme Lord.
The process is easy and efficient
And to the highest success they go toward.

Faith is So Important

Faith is most important
For attaining spiritual success.
Right association helps us
In establishing firm progress.

Our faith in devotional service
Can give us all perfection.
Our humility with acceptance
Helps us depend on the Lord's protection.

Faithless men don't reach
Toward human life's ultimate goal.
They remain in illusion
By imprisoning their very own soul.

No light of hope exists
In the way of faithlessness.
So faith is so important
To revive God consciousness.

The Divine Qualities

Godly men are endowed
With divine qualities and nature.
They have fearlessness, vigor, purification
And compassion for every creature.

Free of anger, greed and envy
They lead a life of austerity.
Nonviolence, truthfulness, calmness
And eager to give in charity.

Forgiveness, modesty, simplicity
Always abide in their attitude.
They possess the priceless jewels
Of gentleness, modesty and fortitude.

Self-control, sacrifice, tranquility,
Study of scriptures, cleanliness, renunciation,
No passion for their personal honor–
They're decorated with steady determination.

Cultivation of knowledge blesses
Godly men with perfect consciousness.
Elevation on the highest path of purity
Takes them to the goal of all happiness.

Rare Qualities

Knowledge bestows the rare quality
Of being unwavering and controlled.
The steady sage looks with an equal eye
On a lump of earth, a stone and gold.

He accepts wanted or unwanted situations
Knowing that the modes alone are active.
He's always neutral, content and tranquil
Without being sad, dismal or negative.

His mind never wavers between
Honor or dishonor, praise or blame.
By ceasing his material and selfish nature
He treats friend and foe the same.

One in Divine Consciousness

The special soul with divine consciousness
Knows within that he does nothing at all.
Though he sees, hears, smells, touches and moves,
He's spiritually aware to answer the Lord's call.

Though he speaks, sleeps and breathes
And he knows the truth of all acts,
He appears to be working with his senses
But stays aloof from their objects.

A person engaged in God consciousness
Has nothing to do with the labor
That depends on the five immediate, remote causes:
The doer, work, situation, fortune and endeavor.

The Demoniac Nature

Those who are demoniac do not know
What is to be done or elude.
Cleanliness, proper behavior or truthfulness
Do not exist in their attitude.

They say that this world is unreal,
Without foundation, no God in control.
They say it is the production of sex desire
And that's there's no existence of the soul.

Following such conclusions, the demoniac
Are lost and have no intelligence.
They are engaged in unbeneficial, horrible works
Meant to destroy the worldly existence.

The demoniac are sworn to unclean works,
Engaged in false prestige and pride.
Thus illusioned, attracted by the impermanent,
They take shelter of lust which is never satisfied.

Their firm belief is that sense gratification
Is human civilization's prime necessity.
Thus until the end of their life,
There is no end to their anxiety.

Bound by a network of millions of desires
And absorbed in anger and lust,
They secure money by illegal means
And in God, they have no trust.

Demons think, so much wealth do I have
And I will gain more than before.
So much opulence is mine now
And I shall increase it more and more.

He is my enemy and I have killed him
And my other enemies will be killed.
I am the lord of everything;
My desire for enjoyment will be fulfilled.

I am perfect, powerful, rich and happy,
I am surrounded by relatives far and wide.
No one is so powerful and happy as I;
Doing sacrifices and giving charity; I feel pride.

Perplexed by various anxieties
And bound by a network of illusions,
Demoniac persons fall down into darkness
Thinking that sense pleasures are the solution.

Demons deluded by wealth and false prestige,
Self-complacent and neglecting rules and regulations;
Sometimes they proudly perform sacrifices
Only for their name and reputations.

Bewildered by false ego, strength,
Lust, anger, blasphemy and pride,
The demons become envious of the Lord
Not caring for Who is inside.

The Blue Lord

The blue Lord's lotus feet
Provide shelter to all.
His protection is certain
No matter how big or how small.

The blue Lord's lotus hands
Bestow unlimited gifts.
If one falls down in the dark
His hands are there to lift.

The lotus-eyed blue Lord
Always showers His compassion.
His cooling sight soothes
Anger, greed, ego and passion.

The Glorious Lord

O, Lord of all beings–
Your merciful glance dissipates
The deep darkness of ignorance.
Once we are enlightened,
We see in all beings Your presence.

O, Supreme Person–
You open Your shelter for everyone
Being our foremost friend.
Just as clouds pour rain over all,
Be it on the ocean or dry land.

O, all-pervading Lord–
You create and maintain the universe
By Your divine power and opulence.
Even a blade of grass can't move
Without Your will and excellence.

O, Supreme Personality of Godhead–
Everything rests upon Your supremacy
As pearls are strung on a thread.
There is no truth superior to You;
Your presence in every atom is spread.

I Am . . .

I am the all-pervading Supersoul
Who is seated in everyone's heart.
I am the end of all beings–
Their middle and their start.

Of all the lights
I am the radiant sunlight
And among the stars
I'm the moon at night.

Of the senses I'm the mind
And I guide one on the right course.
And in all living beings
I am the living force.

Of bodies of water, I'm the ocean,
Of trees I'm the banyan tree,
Among subduers, I am time;
The Himalayan mountains represent Me.

Of all the many sacrifices,
I am the chanting of the holy name.
And among all women,
I am fortune, fine speech and fame.

Of elephants, I'm Airavata,
Among cows I am surabhi.
I'm the month of November
And of poems, I'm the Gayatri.

I am the thunderbolt of all weapons
And the shark among the fish.
I am the generating principle;
Everything works according to My wish.

I am the God of love, Kandarpa,
The cause for all procreation.
I am also Lord Brahma,
The creator of the creation.

I am the holy Ganges River
Among the rivers that flow by.
I am the strong, gusty wind
And all things I purify.

Of all the sciences,
I am the proof.
And among logicians
I'm the conclusive truth.

Of letters, I'm the letter A.
Among words, I'm the dual compound.
Of seasons, flower-bearing spring
And am 'om' among all the sounds.

I am the splendid of the splendor
And all victory and adventure.
I am all-devouring death–
The end of every creature.

Of the wielders of weapons
I am Rama, the Supreme Savior.
Of the five Pandavas,
I am Arjuna, the great warrior.

I am the wisdom of the wise
And the strength among the strong.
I am punishment for those
Who have done things wrong.

Among men who seek victory
I am morality.
Of secret things I'm silence
And the wisdom of all that be.

I am the generating seed
Of every existence that shall be.
Moving and nonmoving beings
Cannot exist without Me.

There is no end
To my divine manifestation.
All that I have explained of My opulences
Is but a mere indication.

Know that all My opulence
And My beautiful and glorious creation
Springs from but a spark
Of My splendid situation.

What need is there
For all these detailed verses?
With just a single fragment of Myself
I pervade and support all universes.

God's Identity

God is the taste of water
And the light of the moon and sun.
He's the syllable 'om' in the mantras
And the ability in everyone.

He is the fragrance of the earth
And the heat in the fiery blazes.
He is the life of all that lives
And the penances of all the sages.

He is the prowess of all powerful men
And the original seed of existence.
He is also the strength of the strong
And the root of all one's intelligence.

The Supreme Person

One must meditate on the Supreme Person
Who knows past, present and future.
He is not impersonal or void
But is the creator of all creatures.

He is older than the oldest
And the origin of all things.
He is luminous like the sun
And radiant light He brings.

He is smaller than the smallest
And can enter into an atomic part.
He controls as the Supersoul
Being seated in everyone's heart.

He is inconceivable and the sustainer
And beyond all material conception.
He is always a transcendental person
And the maintainer of every manifestation.

The Lord's Energies

I am the father of this universe,
Mother, support and the great sire;
I am the holy chant, sacrifice, ritual,
Healthy herb, butter, offering and fire.

I am the object of knowledge,
The purifier and syllable 'om'.
I am the offering to ancestors
The Vedas manifest from Me alone.

I am the goal, sustainer, master and witness,
The abode, refuge and the most dear friend.
I am the basis of everything, the resting place,
The eternal seed, both the beginning and the end.

I give heat and torrents of rain,
I am the cause of clouds to swell.
Both spirit and matter come from Me
And immortality and death as well.

Inferior and Superior Energies

Earth, water, fire, air and ether,
Intelligence, false ego and mind;
The Lord's separated material energies–
All together–there are eight kinds.

Besides these, another is His superior energy
Which comprises the spirit soul
Who is exploiting the material nature
And is always under the Lord's control.

All beings have their source in these two natures–
Either material or spiritual in this creation.
The Lord is the cause of all causes
And is both the origin and dissolution.

The Dutiful Lord

Within all planets–higher or lower–
There is no work required for Me.
Nor have I want or need of anything,
Yet I discharge My duty with glee.

If I ever failed to do My work
And not follow the prescribed aims,
All the people of the world
Certainly would do the same.

If I did not perform My duties,
All worlds would be put to ruination.
I would destroy the peace of all beings
And would be the cause of unwanted population.

The All-Pervading Lord

The splendor of the sun, moon and fire
Come from Me and dissipate the darkness.
These emanate by My causeless mercy
To bless all with energy and brightness.

I enter into all planets;
They stay in orbit by My might.
To supply the juice to vegetables,
I enter into the moonlight.

I join with the air of life
As it enters and retreats.
I'm the fire of digestion for all,
To digest the food they eat.

I am seated in everyone's heart;
Remembrance and forgetfulness come from Me.
I am the knower of the Vedas
And all the Vedas are compiled by Me.

The possession of the material body
Is temporary and fragile in nature.
So lamentation is of no worth
Over such an impermanent creature.

The Supersoul

The Supersoul exists in His all-pervading form
As the sun diffuses its rays.
Everywhere are His hands, legs, eyes, head and face,
But the individual soul is not situated in this way.

Although He is the source of all senses,
He has no material senses like we.
He is detached although the maintainer of all
And transcendental to all that be.

He exists outside and inside of all beings
Whether moving or non-moving animal or plant.
By the power of our limited material senses,
We try to see and know Him but can't.

He is situated as one and never divided
Although seemingly divided among all.
He is the maintainer of all living entities;
It is understood, He devours and develops all.

He is the goal and object of knowledge
And situated in everyone's heart.
He is the source of light in luminous objects,
Is unmanifested and beyond the dark.

Because He's described it in summary,
The devotees can understand
The field of activities, knowledge and knowable
And thus attain His eternal land.

Changing Bodies

A person changes his body at each moment–
From childhood to youth to old age.
When a person leaves his body,
A sober one is not bewildered by this stage.

At the time of death, the soul leaves the body
And accepts another according to his actions.
He then gets a temporary, material body
Depending upon his karmic reactions.

If one, however, gives up his body
While remembering the Supreme Lord,
He is then transported to the spiritual world,
Reaching the goal that he's worked toward.

There is no endurance of the material body
And there is no change of the eternal soul.
This is the conclusion of all seers of the truth–
The difference between the part and the whole.

Body and Soul

A wise one knows what is body and soul,
Not lamenting for the living or deceased.
Knowledge illuminates the consciousness
And one's peacefulness is then increased.

No birth and death for the eternal soul
Who is ever-existing, primeval and unborn.
So with the destruction of the temporary body,
There is no cause to lament or to mourn.

The soul can't be cut, dried, or withered
Nor moistened or burned by a flame.
He is immovable, insoluble, invisible,
Unchangeable and eternally the same.

The soul is always full with consciousness
Being part and parcel of the Supreme Whole.
He is indestructible, inconceivable, ever-lasting–
And we are not this body but spirit soul.

The Embodied Spirit Soul

When a living being controls his nature,
Mentally renouncing his active state,
He can come out of the bodily conception
And happily reside in the city of nine gates.

The spirit, the master of the city of his body,
Doesn't create activities or the fruits of actions.
All is enacted by the modes of material nature;
He is not the controller of his actions and reactions.

The embodied spirit is bewildered by ignorance
And is then put into certain conditions.
Thus the chain of action and reaction continues
But the Lord is not responsible for those actions.

The Body's Destiny

We are not that body
But the eternal spirit soul.
We are but a fragment
Of the eternal, Supreme Whole.

The body appears for a while
Then disappears forever.
To try to make it everlasting
Is not a worthwhile endeavor.

Every living body is made
Of the worldly elements.
It returns to dust in the end
Thus ceasing all life's events.

The possession of the material body
Is temporary and fragile in nature.
So lamentation has no worth
For such an impermanent creature.

Wearing Another Body

The living entity carries his conceptions
As aromas are carried in the air.
After he quits his present body,
A different body he will wear.

Each body obtains different types
Of taste, smell, touch, sound and sight.
They are grouped together about the mind
Allowing one to enjoy sensual delights.

Fools cannot see how the soul changes bodies
And how they enjoy under the spell of nature.
Those whose eyes are trained in knowledge
Can see the suffering of every creature.

Striving transcendentalists can see
That the soul is eternal and does not die.
But those not situated in self-realization
Can not see this, though they may try.

The Body's Nature

Bodies are born, grow and are here for a while,
Produce some by products and decay.
They pass through the six stages
And then reach their final day.

One who understands the body's nature
Is called the knower of the bodily field.
The knowledge of it and its activities
Are in various Vedas revealed.

Whatever we see in this existence
Of both the moving and non-moving objects
Is just a combination of the knower,
Of the field and its various acts.

One who sees the Supersoul
Along with the soul everywhere,
Who understands that both can't be destroyed
He can actually see; that is rare.

One who sees the Supersoul's presence in every being
And does not degrade himself by his mind,
Is illuminated by this knowledge
And the transcendental destination he finds.

Not Lamenting for any Changes

Winter turns to summer
Sorrow turns to delight,
Youth changes into old age
Day changes into night.

Old age meets its end,
End starts with a new aim.
The worldly nature always changes
But spirit stays the same.

So learned ones never lament
For the living or the dead.
They firmly follow the path
And go back home, 'Back to Godhead'.

The Final Destiny

All beings remain unmanifest
Before their beginning in the sphere.
Unmanifested when annihilated
Only in the middle they appear.

Their bodies are created by five elements:
Ether, air, fire, water and earth.
Their final destiny goes back to these
So lamentation has no worth.

The material elements don't manifest
Before the cosmic creation.
From the subtle state of being
Comes non-manifestation and manifestation.

Just as
From ether, air is generated.
From air, fire is activated.
From fire, water is generated.
From water, earth is cultivated.

Things are manifested or unmanifested
In the due course of time and tide.
No reason to lament in either stage;
One should stay stable on each side.

Our Consciousness at the Final Test

A wrinkled body that's near its end
Has no bright hope anymore.
Its breath is going to cease
When death stands at the door.

Life's journey has now passed
Dreams have flown away,
Dark shadows take life over
Departing from the living day.

Our thoughts are on the moment,
Reflecting on the past.
It's not easy to change
Our consciousness at the last.

The Lord gave us the chance
To pass the final test.
Preparation must be perfect
To attain the result that's best.

The human form of life
Is an opportunity for devotion.
If we learn our lesson well,
There will no longer be demotion.

The Reality of the World

Grief-stricken families remain behind
After the departure of their dearest one.
Everything turns into deep darkness;
There's not even a single ray of the sun.

This material world is temporary,
Full with suffering and full with pain.
To get everlasting happiness here–
It's not possible to find or attain.

The Journey

The journey that goes between
Our life of birth and death
Will teach us many lessons
With each and every breath.

A single step becomes a struggle
If we go onto the wrong track.
The time that has already passed–
That time will never come back.

The journey becomes joyous
If we follow the right path.
Service to the Creator and created
Ceases all worldly wrath.

Preparation for the Next Destination

Whoever at the end of his life
Remembers Me and is devout.
He attains My transcendental nature–
Of this, there is no doubt.

Whatever state one remembers
At the end when death prevails,
He will attain that same state
Spiritual or material without fail.

Therefore, one must always think of Me
And dedicate his activities to Me.
Once his mind and intelligence are fixed,
He will certainly come to Me.

The Highest Perfection

One who, at the time of death,
Remembers the Supreme with devotion,
And with the help of his lifetime practice,
Will attain the ultimate promotion.

Bhakti-yoga and chanting the holy name–
Such a combination helps one to think of Me.
An undeviating mind at death takes
His journey straight back to Me.

He who thinks of Me without deviation,
Controlling his thoughts from other notions,
Obtains Me much more easily
Through his constant service in devotion.

Such a great soul never returns
To this temporary world full of pains.
He reaches Me, The Supreme Lord,
And there is no higher perfection to attain.

The Result of Self-Control

Basic demands of the body:
Eating, sleeping, defending and mating.
With no restraint of one's habits,
Good fortune will not be waiting.

The prison house of the senses
Binds one to the slavery chain.
He meets a pale, dry autumn
Missing all spiritual gain.

A self-controlled and firm person
Remains stable in every game.
As a lamp in a windless place
Burns on with a steady flame.

One on the Imperishable Path

One who doesn't give to others
Any difficulty or disturbance
Is not disturbed by anyone
And lives a life of tolerance.

He never tries to make his way
Depending on ordinary activities.
He is pure, expert and equally poised
And a friend to all living entities.

He honors others with gratitude
Treating them as the Lord's parts.
His actions please the Supreme One
And from good fortune he never departs.

He sets an enlivening example
For the welfare of society.
His steps on the imperishable path
Make him very dear to the Almighty.

Tolerating All Situations

Dark distress turns to blooming happiness
As winter turns to summer season.
They arise from sense perception;
To be disturbed; there is no reason.

Their arrival and departure are not forever;
One must tolerate both situations.
Such steady souls are eligible
To achieve everlasting liberation.

Seeing with Equal Visison

The omnipresent Lord
Exists in everyone's heart.
He's the Supreme Father of all;
Everyone is His dear part.

One in God consciousness doesn't make
Distinction between species and caste.
Seeing with equal vision, all as the same:
Cow, dog, elephant, learned or outcast.

All bodies are material productions,
Different modes of material nature,
Yet the soul within the body is the same
And God is equal to every creature.

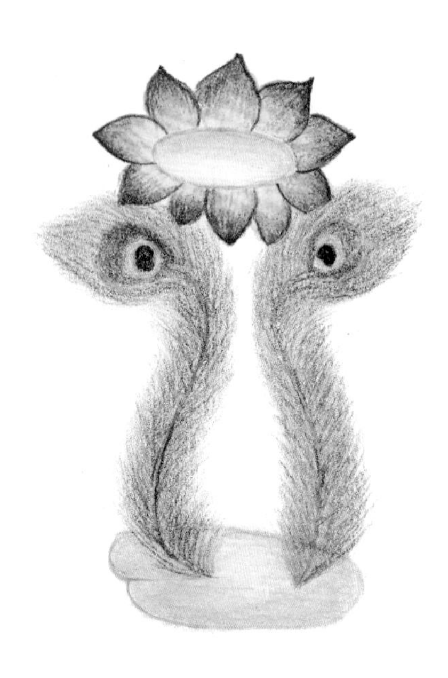

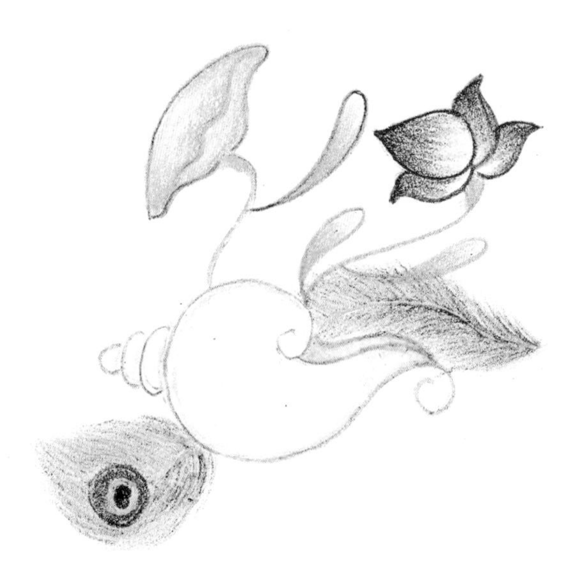

The Path to Freedom

All our actions for sense pleasure
Are influenced by deep ignorance.
Pure love for the Lord helps us
To get out from our suffering existence.

Renouncing one's actions do not purify
The heart of a conditioned soul.
But acting in God consciousness–
His senses are under control.

One who never hates or hankers
For the fruits of his activities
Fortunately gets freedom from
Material bondage and dualities.

The Only Solution

The real cause of suffering
Is hankering for sense gratification.
The bodily conception of life
Keeps us in deep lamentation.

Material efforts are all useless–
It's like holding water in a sieve.
Material life is like a mirage
And there's nothing we can achieve.

Our journey is ever endless
As we travel from one to another lifetime.
In this temporary material world,
Nothing is permanent or sublime.

The only solution here
Is that our senses should be under control.
The way is very simple
If we serve the Supreme Soul.

The Lord's Dear Devotees

One who is not envious of others
But is a kind friend to everyone–
Such a devotee is very dear to Me
As he has no false ego from what he's done.

One who does not think himself a proprietor
And is calm in difficulty or progress–
Such a devotee is very dear to Me
As he's equal in happiness and distress.

One who is tolerant, satisfied and self-controlled
And does devotional service with determination–
Such a devotee is very dear to Me
As he has all transcendental qualifications.

One who is not disturbed by anyone
And never puts others into difficulty–
Such a devotee is very dear to Me
As he's equipoised in fear and anxiety.

One who doesn't depend on ordinary activities,
Who is pure, expert and free from all pain–
Such a devotee is very dear to Me
As he doesn't strive for any gain.

One who neither rejoices nor grieves
For pleasures or pain–whatever life brings–
Such a devotee is very dear to Me
As he renounces auspicious or inauspicious things.

One who treats a friend and a foe alike
And is equipoised in praise and blame–
Such a devotee is very dear to Me
As he's equal in infamy and in fame.

One who is always satisfied with anything
And is free from contaminating association–
Such a devotee is very dear to Me
As he's fixed in knowledge and realization.

One who follows this imperishable path
And renders devotional service faithfully–
Such a devotee is very dear to Me
As he makes Me the supreme goal, doubtlessly.

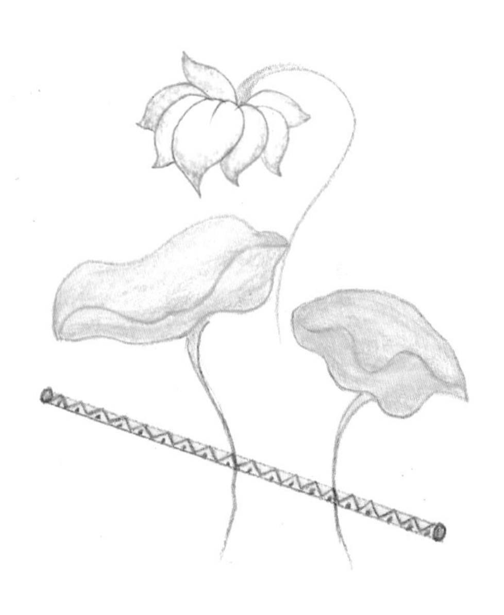

The Elevated Stage

Giving up sense enjoyment,
Also being purified,
Being freed from attachment and hatred,
One becomes self-satisfied.

He who lives in a secluded place
And controls his tongue, body, speech and mind,
Is always in trance and is peaceful –
Within him, false ego you'll not find.

Free from false strength, lust and attachment,
From false proprietorship and rage,
Free from acceptance of material things–
Such a person is elevated to the self-realized stage.

Working For Me

A devotee doesn't live on the material plane
But lives in Me, The Supreme Personality.
So you should engage your intelligence in Me
And will associate with Me without difficulty.

If you fail to fix your mind upon Me,
Then follow the devotional rules and regulations.
Develop a desire to attain Me
Under the spiritual master's directions.

You should try to work for Me–
If you cannot, practice the regulations.
Working for My satisfaction and pleasure
You will certainly attain perfection.

If you are unable to work for Me,
Then give up results of your actions.
If you sacrifice for the supreme cause
You will be self-situated in all transactions.

Renunciation of the result of your actions
Surpasses all knowledge and meditation.
Such renunciation brings peace of mind
And step-by-step takes you to your destination.

My Guarantee

My words can never be explained
To those not devoted and austere,
Nor to those who are envious of Me
Who are faithless and not ready to hear.

One who explains My sacred words
To the special souls–to the devotees–
To him pure service is guaranteed
And at the end, he will come to Me.

There is no servant of Mine
Who is and will be more dear
As one who spreads My words
And makes the meanings clear.

I declare here to all:
One who studies this conversation
Worships Me by his intelligence
And attains the highest elevation.

One who listens with faith
And puts all envy aside
Will be free from all reactions
And goes where the pious reside.

My Declaration

All these I declare to be knowledge
And anything else is ignorance:
Approaching a bona fide spiritual master,
Nonviolence, pridelessness and tolerance.

Outward and inward cleanliness,
Accepting every situation with humility,
Steadiness, self-control, renunciation,
Absence of false ego, endowed with simplicity.

Always even-minded
Amid pleasant and unpleasant events,
Constant and unalloyed devotion to Me,
Feeling peaceful and content.

Perception of the four bodily miseries:
Birth, death, disease and old age,
Freedom from worldly entanglements,
Then coming to the transcendental stage.

Detachment from the mass of people,
Aspiring to live in a solitary place,
Accepting the importance of self-realization
And trying to attain My eternal place.

Perfect Realization

One who controls the various senses
Who is equal to every entity,
And worships the impersonal conception,
Will achieve Me, the Supreme Personality.

To perceive the Supersoul in the individual soul,
One has to cease all sensual activities.
Loving service to Me is required
To understand My presence in all living entities.

Realizing this, he envies no one
And with respect offers a feast.
Perfect realization blesses him to see
No difference between man and beast.

The Real Freedom

One can get real freedom
From the bondage of all sin.
One requires many lessons;
It's never too late to begin.

Working so hard to please the Lord
With all of our devotion
Will stop all of our suffering
In the deep, material ocean.

Our loving devotional service
Eliminates all reactions.
Devout activities deliver
A chance for some purification.

A pure God-conscious, eternal life
Bestows self-realization.
One cannot ascertain the truth
Through mental speculation.

The modest devotional life
Is a good move toward one's freedom.
One eventually enters into
The Lord's eternal kingdom.

The Importance of Equality

Life is not a bed of roses;
With every step there are changes.
But barriers can be crossed
If we accept what the Lord arranges.

Acceptance of a new change starts
By following the right ways.
Compassion for the whole living race
Is like the sun distributing its rays.

The Lord's Appearance

As the Lord of all living entities,
My body's eternal and unborn.
I still appear in every millennium
In My original, transcendental form.

Whenever and wherever
The religious practice starts to bend
And there is a predominance of irreligion,
At that time I Myself descend.

To annihilate the miscreants
And to deliver the pious sage,
To reestablish the principles of religion,
I Myself appear in every age.

One who knows the transcendental nature
Of My appearance and every activity,
Takes no further birth in the material world
But attains My abode of eternity.

Some Can't Understand Me

This material nature is one of My energies,
Working under My will and direction.
Producing all moving and non-moving beings
I create and annihilate this manifestation.

When I descend in the human form,
Fools cannot detect and ascertain Me.
They don't know My transcendental nature
As the Supreme Lord of all that be.

Such bewildered souls are attracted
By demoniac and atheistic situations.
All their projects and plans are defeated
As are their activities, knowledge and hopes for liberation.

Advanced Souls

Advanced souls do their work
Caring not for defeat or for gain.
Always honoring their regular duty
They're not attached to joy or to pain.

They find all satisfaction within
Keeping external illusions away.
They rise to higher plateaus
Achieving success along the way.

The Importance of Regulation

If one is in perfect discipline
Following the path of regulation,
He will climb a sublime mountain
And reach the highest elevation.

Regulating his eating and sleeping
Helps to set one in pure existence.
Too much or too little routine
Doesn't make for a fruitful subsistence.

When controlling all eating and sleeping
As well as activities and play,
The darkness will stay at a distance;
Brightness will shine every day.

The Way to liberation

One whose happiness is inward,
Who is active and rejoicing within,
Always working for others' welfare–
He is always freed from all sin.

One beyond dualities and doubt,
Who surpasses anger and materialism,
Achieves supreme liberation
And is self-realized in perfect mysticism.

The Future of the Unsuccessful Yogi

Yogis meet with no destruction
In this world or in the next.
Evil can not touch those who are
Surrendered and not perplexed.

Even the unsuccessful yogi
Reappears in a family who is righteous.
As past pious deeds deliver him
To a life that is quite prosperous.

Appearing in a family of devotees
Is a most fortunate birth.
Being able to make this progress
Is a rare chance on this Earth.

The Yoga Ladder

Linking oneself with the Supreme Lord
Is yoga and called renunciation.
No one can be a yogi unless
He gives up desires for sense gratification.

This process may be compared to a ladder
Where one can attain the top realization.
Beginning from the lowest material condition
One rises up to spiritual perfection.

One who always meditates on the Lord
Ceasing all disturbing mental activities,
Who is constantly engaged in the Lord's service,
Is purified from all material proclivities.

How to be the Topmost Yogi

A yogi should always engage his body,
Mind and self with the Supreme.
Free from desires, feelings of possessiveness
He should cease all mundane dreams.

He should always remain in seclusion
To avoid disturbance from external objects.
He should accept favorable conditions for realization
And anything unfavorable, he should reject.

All instructions are here by the Lord
In how to engage in our pursuits.
By loving service and thoughts of the Lord,
The yogi attains the sweetest fruits.

Attracted to the Yogic Ways

One becomes attracted to the yogic ways
Through virtue of his divine life before.
Such an inquisitive transcendentalist.
Need not to follow the rituals any more.

His endeavors wash all contamination
And purify his very soul.
Through practice after many, many births
He attains the supreme goal.

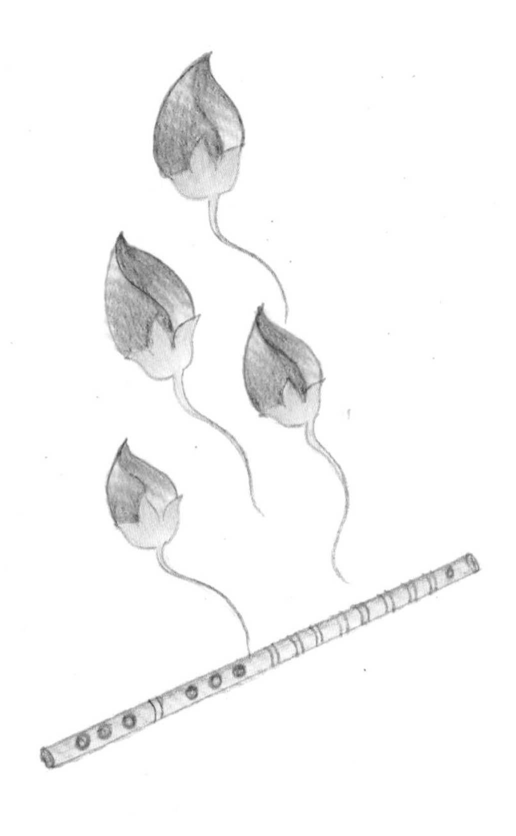

The Aim of Yoga

Yoga means to meditate on Me
And at the same time to be occupied.
The whole aim is to satisfy Me,
Thus everyone will be satisfied.

Like watering the root of a tree,
All leaves and branches get satisfaction.
In My pure devotional service,
One can experience all gratification.

Performing Our Prescribed Duties

When we perform our prescribed duties
Without attachment to failure or success,
Our evenness and peace of mind
Leads us on the path of spiritual progress.

If we do many good deeds
Without desiring the fruits,
Our acts will purify us
So we can serve the Absolute.

Misers not employing their energy
In the service of the Lord,
Enjoy the results of their works
And become bound to the material cord.

The devotional service to the Almighty
Is the right course of our action.
Ever-disturbed senses can be controlled
By working for the Lord's satisfaction.

Doing One's Own Duty

A man who performs his own work
Can surely attain perfection
By worshiping the Supreme Lord
Who pervades in all directions.

It is better to do one's own duty
Though it may need some correction.
One should not accept another's duty
Even though performed with perfection.

Every endeavor is covered by fault
As smoke is covered by fire.
So one should do his natural duty
Even if rectification is required.

Special Mercy

My devotees' thoughts dwell in Me.
They fully serve Me all the time.
Conversing about Me with each other,
They feel blissful, enlightened and sublime.

Those who serve Me constantly
With love, devotion and glee,
I give them the understanding
By which they can come to Me.

Showing them My special mercy,
I, dwelling in their hearts,
With the shining lamp of knowledge
I destroy their dark, ignorant parts.

Transcendentally Situated

When one is transcendentally situated,
He realizes the Lord and is in ecstasy.
Being equal to all and without misery and desires,
He attains pure devotional service to Me.

Service in devotion is the way
To enter into My eternal abode.
When one is fully conscious of Me,
He can understand Me as God.

Though engaged in different activities
While under My shield of protection,
My pure devotees reach My realm,
The imperishable home of all perfection.

The Divine Protection

Great souls who are not deluded
Are always under the protection of My divinity.
They are fully engaged in devotional service
Knowing Me as the original, inexhaustible Personality.

Always chanting My glories and chanting My name,
Always bowing down and knowing the way;
These great souls worship Me with love
Endeavoring with determination every day.

Goodness, Passion and Ignorance

Coming from the mode of goodness,
Real knowledge and happiness are activated.
They raise one to the higher planets
Where everyone is highly elevated.

From the mode of passion develops
Miseries, distress, avarice and greed.
One remains on the earthly planets
Frustrated trying to satisfy desires and needs.

From the mode of ignorance develops
Foolishness, madness and illusion.
It pushes one down to the hellish worlds
Where one remains in the darkest delusion.

How One is Recognized

When these modes compete for supremacy–
Goodness, passion and ignorance–
One can then be recognized
By that particular mode's prominence.

The manifestation of goodness illuminates
All gates of the body with perception.
Then by the power of goodness
Every gate develops the right conception.

Passion creates hankering, many desires,
Dissatisfaction from achievement.
One craves gratification without cessation
And doesn't get happiness, just bereavement.

When ignorance rules over one's life,
Darkness, inertia, madness and illusion prevail.
He makes no endeavor for the right purpose,
Thus, his position remains inactive and pale.

Foods

Foods in goodness please the heart
Giving strength, happiness and satisfaction.
Juicy, wholesome foods bring health
Increasing purity and life's duration.

Too bitter, salty, hot, pungent foods
Are dear to those in passion.
Such foods cause distress, misery and disease
Creating an unhealthy, unpleasing reaction.

Those who are in darkness like foods
That are tasteless, putrid and old.
Such foods give them no happiness
As their senses are uncontrolled.

The Worker

Goodness blesses the worker with enthusiasm
Who is humble with great determination.
He doesn't waver in success or failure
But performs his duty without material association.

A worker in passion is greedy, impure
And moved by happiness and pain.
He's always envious, attached to materialism
And works only for his personal gain.

A worker in ignorance defies the scriptures.
He is lazy, morose and obstinate.
Expert in cheating and insulting others,
He does not fail to procrastinate.

Renunciation

Renunciation in the mode of goodness
Means always perform duties as prescribed.
Giving up all material association
And attachment to the results that work provides.

Giving up duties out of trouble or out of fear
Means renunciation in the mode of passion.
If a person renounces work in that spirit,
His actions never lead to elevation.

Renunciation in the mode of ignorance
Means to give up duties because of illusion.
Disregarding one's sense of work
Is out of darkness and confusion.

Happiness

Happiness in the mode of goodness
Is just like poison at first.
It awakens one to self-realization in the end
And becomes nectar and quenches one's thirst.

Happiness in the mode of passion
Is like nectar at the start.
The senses and their objects find it pleasing
But the result is poison when joy departs.

Happiness in the mode of ignorance
Deludes one from beginning to termination;
It comes from sleep, laziness and illusion
And blinds one to self-realization.

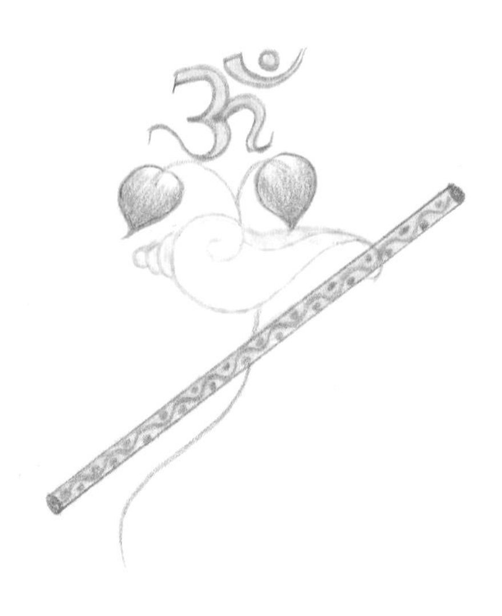

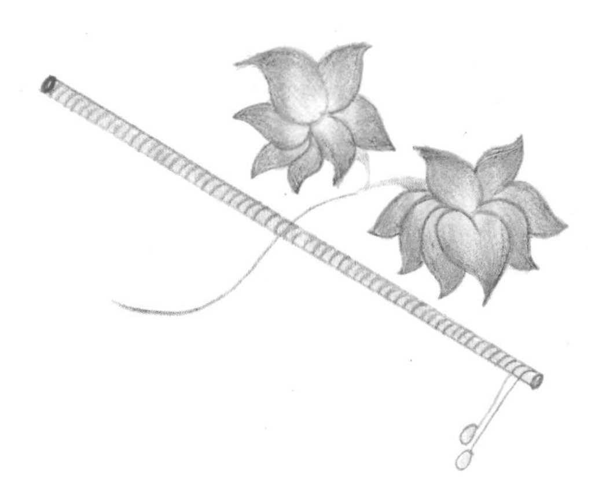

Action

Action in the mode of goodness
Is regulated and is sane.
Free from love or hatred
Without desire for fruitive gain.

Acting in the mode of passion
One acts from false ego and pride.
He searches for sense gratification
But his efforts are dissatisfied.

Action in the mode of ignorance
Causes one to disregard scriptural injunctions.
He's unconcerned for future bondage
Or others' distress or destruction.

Charity

Charity in the mode of goodness
Given with no expectation of return,
At the proper time, place and to a worthy person,
Is given out of duty, with sincere concern.

Charity is in the mode of passion
When given with a selfish motivation,
With a propensity to get a reward
Or given under social obligation.

Charity in the mode of ignorance
Is given at an improper time without attention,
At an impure place, to an unworthy person;
That charity is a useless invention.

Understanding

Understanding in the mode of goodness teaches
What should be done and what should not.
The difference between liberation and bondage
One learns what is fearful and what is not.

Understanding in passion covers all distinctions
Between religious and irreligious deeds.
One cannot make any difference between the actions
With which one should and should not proceed.

Ignorant understanding works in the wrong way
Under the spell of illusion and darkness.
Considering religion is sin and sin is religion,
One ends in the darkest consciousness.

Determination

Determination in goodness is well-sustained,
Steadfast, unbreakable, and non-deviated.
It controls the mind, the life and the senses
And life's fortune is then elevated.

Determination in passion holds
Deep desire for the fruitful reward.
Economy and sense gratification arise
In one's consciousness and self-regard.

One's determination in ignorance does not surpass
Dreaming, fearfulness, and lamentation.
Moroseness and illusion make their way
Through unintelligent mental speculation.

Knowledge

Knowledge in goodness gives vision
To see in all the spiritual nature.
Though they have different forms,
The Lord resides in every creature.

With knowledge in passion one sees differences
Between the bodies of different living entities.
One sees only the outside form and shape,
Not the inner soul with this mentality.

Knowledge in ignorance covers wisdom
Making one think meager and small.
By missing the light of the truth,
One sees his work as all in all.

Penance

Penance performed in goodness
Means acts performed without material motivation.
They are done only for the sake of the Supreme
With transcendental faith and determination.

Penance performed in passion
For pride, honor, and admiration
Is not stable or permanent
And is of short duration.

Penance done out of foolishness,
To injure or destroy another's existence,
Will also cause distress for oneself
And such penance is in the mode of ignorance.

Sacrifice

Sacrifice is in the mode of goodness
When done according to scriptural injunctions.
It is done as a matter of duty
Without desire for rewards of actions.

When sacrifice is performed by a person
To achieve some material possession,
Or if one does it out of pride,
That sacrifice is in the mode of passion.

Sacrifice in ignorance means it is
Without Vedic hymns and distribution of a feast.
It's done without faith and regard to the scriptures
Or without rewarding or remunerating the priest.

Death

Death in the mode of goodness
Allows one to die in a good, conscious stage.
He'll attain the higher planets
Of the pure devotee and great sage.

Death in passion means a birth among
Those engaged in material activity.
He works so hard for sensual pleasures
Yet never reaches his desired destiny.

In ignorance, death fixes the destination
To a lower birth in the animal kingdom.
Struggling always for existence,
And so far from spiritual freedom.

Action and Inaction

Even an intelligent one is bewildered to know
What is action and what is inaction.
The Supreme Lord explains the difference
To liberate us from an unfortunate situation.

It is hard to understand the difference between
What is action, inaction and forbidden action.
The proper knowledge must be awakened
That everyone is connected as the Lord's relation.

A wise one beholds with proper vision
Action in inaction and inaction in action.
He is in the transcendental position
Although engaged in different transactions.

The Banyan Tree

There is an imperishable banyan tree
With its branches down and roots upward.
Its leaves are the Vedic hymns
And the knower of this tree goes forward.

The modes of goodness, passion and ignorance
Nourish this whole banyan tree.
The twigs are the objects of senses with roots down
And are bound to the fruitive actions of society.

No one can understand where this tree ends,
Where it begins or where is its foundation.
One must cut down this strongly-rooted tree
With the weapons of detachment and determination.

The material world is like a banyan tree
Where fruitive activities have no end.
One wanders from one branch to another;
Still he doesn't find his eternal friend.

Therefore, one must seek such a place
From which, having gone, one never returns.
This is the Supreme Lord's eternal abode,
The place for which we all yearn.

He who surrenders to the Supreme Personality,
From whom everything begins and extends,
Can cut down this false, reflected tree
And attain the real tree of the spiritual land.

A Different use of Time

When common men sleep
The self-controlled souls arise.
When the common men awaken
It's night for the learned and wise.

When the common men remain unconscious
In the lap of the full nighttime,
The self-realized souls wake up
And make their consciousness sublime.

The common men work hard
For sense pleasure in the daylight.
The earnest sages remain alert
To protect their spiritual sight.

The Five Factors of Action

The body and the performer,
And the senses and transactions
Along with the Supersoul:
These are the five factors of action.

Right or wrong, whatever one performs
With body, speech or mind,
Is caused by these five factors:
The Supreme directly has defined.

One who doesn't consider these five
But thinks himself the performing star;
He is in lack of good intelligence
And cannot see things as they are.

Austerity

Austerity of the body means
Respecting the Supreme, superiors and teachers.
Being clean, simple, celibate, peaceful
And free from violence towards all creatures.

The austerity of speech is given
As words that please the ear.
Speaking truthfully and beneficially
Reciting scriptures to bring cheer.

Austerities of the mind are described
As satisfaction, self-control and purity.
Shining through one's thoughts and deeds,
One works with gravity and simplicity.

The Key to Success

Knowledge, the object of knowledge and the knower
Are the three factors that motivate action.
The senses, the work and the doer
Are the three constituents of that action.

One will undergo thinking, feeling and willing
Before he starts any transaction.
Any work that he does has these three elements
And his impetus is called inspiration.

The inspiration to work is sublime
If it comes from scriptural injunction.
The worker will achieve success of his deeds
If he follows the spiritual master's instruction.

The Boat of Knowledge

Once one is in the boat of knowledge,
The ocean of miseries he can cross.
Even the most sinful of all sinners
Is saved from the greatest loss.

Perfect knowledge of the self and the Lord
And understanding this relationship as he should,
Burns all reactions to material activities
As a fire makes ashes out of wood.

Such knowledge is the fruit of all mysticism
Proving itself to be incomparably sublime
And one who practices it in devotional service,
Enjoys transcendence in due course of time.

One in Full Knowledge

One is understood to be in full knowledge
Whose actions are devoid of sense desire.
He is said by sages to be a worker
Whose reactions are burnt up by wisdom's fire.

He is free from all attachments
To the results of work in which he's engaged.
He performs no fruitive action
And attains the most satisfying stage.

He acts only for the bare necessities
With controlled intelligence and mind.
He gives up proprietorship over possessions
And is not affected by reactions of any kind.

Real Renunciation

The meaning of real renunciation
Is to give up impurities of the heart.
Once one purifies himself deeply inside,
His inside dirt will immediately depart.

Inner purification illumines one's life
Turning darkness into bright day.
Once the light of knowledge shines,
Dark obscurity goes away.

The real renunciation takes one
On the path of dignified deeds.
He finally reaches the glorious goal
As clear vision helps him succeed.

Real Compassion

There's no value to having compassion
For the dress of a drowning one.
The darkness meets its end
By the appearance of the rising sun.

The real efforts shine brightly
If done in the right direction.
One's endeavor to save the soul
Will bestow the fruits of his action.

There's no happiness for an indoor bird
Just by polishing the cage.
Without watering the roots,
Trees don't reach their full stage.

Self-realization signifies compassion
If placed in the eternal soul.
The fixed concept of the real self
Takes one to the ultimate goal.

Budding Lyrics

The spiritual master is the medium
To connect the spirit soul with the Supersoul.
The divine shelter of his lotus feet
Is the human being's perfect goal.

The Supersoul always accompanies
The individual soul in all situations.
Once the spirit soul realizes His presence,
He serves Him with transcendental vibrations.

The Supreme Lord is full in six qualities:
Beauty, wealth, knowledge, renunciation, power, fame
The living entity is endowed with the same qualities
But the quantity is not the same.

Yogis see all living beings
Belonging to the Supreme that be;
Just as the leaves and branches
Are similarly parts of the tree.

We can't see in darkness
Even with open eyes,
And we can't stop the time
As it very quickly flies.

The Lord is present in everyone's heart
And hurting others means hurting Him.
If we do not rectify our actions,
Our lives will be dark and dim.

Our misfortune or fortune travels
With us in every case.
From one to another lifetime
We reap the results of all that took place.

Fortunate souls take the devotional path
And transcend the birth and death bonds.
Once they take even one step to the Lord,
By taking ten steps, The Supreme responds.

With self-control and constant devotion
One loses material attraction.
Being detached from the false enjoyment
One reaches the highest stage of renunciation.

The man who lives free from sins
Avoiding its unending heavy load,
Follows the way of spiritual life
To enter into the kingdom of God.

Just by the watering the root
The whole tree eventually grows.
His compassion upon the suffering
The Lord's mercy eternally flows.

Material life is just like a dream
When the mind accepts it as reality.
It's the cause of both illusory attraction
And forgetfulness of our spiritual identity.

The lotus garland shines so brightly
When the Lord wears it happily.
The good fortune of a blooming blossom
Never withers but blooms eternally.

The self-sufficient Supreme Personality
Doesn't need anything from anyone.
Still He accepts devotees' offerings
Whose devotional life has then begun.

The Lord's Holy Name is the only exit
To get out from the material existence.
For a permanent abode of all happiness
The Lord's Holy Name is the only entrance.

The attachment for temporary benefits
Is the cause of suffering and lamentation.
No permanent dwelling in sand castles;
The result is destructive devastation.

The devotional process is always a success
Leading to the land of bliss and eternity.
Where all knowledge and peace predominates
And one realizes his original identity.

Arrivals of upheavals is certain
On the path of material existence.
The sage is unaffected in any situation
By his powerful persistence.

Work performed as a sacrifice
For the Lord's satisfaction;
No bondage of work remains
One is freed from all reaction.

The absence of all knowledge
Pushes one to deep distraction.
He ignores the Lord's words
And takes his own direction.

The glorious goal of human life
To develop love for the Lord;
The Supreme arranges all favors
And bestows all blissful rewards.

One who is in perfect knowledge
Always content with simple gain;
He is free from duality and envy
Steady in pleasure and in pain.

Determination for devotional service
Never fails in any circumstance.
One surmounts all material difficulties
And performs the purpose at every chance.

The eternal stage of pure consciousness
Perfect source of satisfaction;
Inner cleanliness manifests outside
And shines in every action.

God-centered actions leave not
Any reaction behind the scene.
Serving God with loving attitude
One is fortunate, sacred and serene.

The path becomes smooth and blissful
If the destination is complete.
The benefits of transcendental actions
Are no further detriment or defeat.

The living entities, due to conditioned life,
Struggle hard with the senses and mind.
Just for the passing joy of sense objects;
Perpetual love they can't find.

Truth is visible to fortunate souls
Whose eyes are trained by wisdom.
The picture is clear, no fog or mist
They belong to the spiritual kingdom.

The enlightened and conditioned souls
Both parts of the Supreme;
The first follows the Lord's instruction
The other only chases a dream.

Excessive efforts for sense pleasures
One invites unlimited perplexity;
By losing the inner peace of mind
One misses the treasure of tranquility.

Life is a hard preparation
To be able to pass at the end.
Death is the final examination
It never gives any chance to mend.

To increase joy and decrease pain–
Everyone tries to his best ability;
The secret key of all success
Is to surrender to God with sincerity.

The law of all our actions
Is the law of cause and effect.
Our future life fully depends on
All the karma we collect.

Water can not be divided
By throwing a stone in the lake.
Misfortune can not touch those
Who to the Lord's shelter they take.

By following the regulative principles
Anyone can achieve perfection.
Regulation, so powerful, on the path–
Guiding all with right direction.

Simply by mental speculations
One can not understand the Lord.
For devotional service is the essence
Recognition of Him–the supreme award.

One who works for the Lord's satisfaction
Treats every living being as a friend.
One who makes Him life's supreme destination,
Certainly achieves Him in the end.

The path of pure activities in one's life
Bestows good fortunes and glorious gain.
The benefits of the divine process
Will never diminish but forever remain.

The Supersoul resides with the individual soul
As witness of our every activity.
The Supreme gives us our full freedom:
To choose the path of demise or eternity.

One who depends upon God's protection
Full of faith, without any doubt;
His security is certain in every step
His way is perfect and devout.

Both worlds–fallible and infallible
Eliminate from the Supreme Personality.
The wise one who understands this in full
Always serve Him with all sincerity.

The great souls without delusion
Stay under the protection of divinity.
Knowing Him as the original and inexhaustible
They lovingly serve the Supreme Personality.

Right work means that work is done
According to the scriptures' direction.
Wrong work is work done against
The principles of the scriptural injunction.

The Supersoul is sitting within
Conducting everyone in proper directions.
Less intelligent persons think
That they're the controller of all actions.

One who knows he's the instrument of work
And that the supreme sanctifier is the Lord,
Is one who is never in illusion
And easily cuts the false egoist cord.

One with the vision of eternity can see
The imperishable soul beyond material nature.
The soul neither does anything nor is entangled
Despite activities with the bodily features.

When one stops seeing the different identities
Due to different bodies of the soul,
He is purified seeing them equally
And attains the transcendental goal.

One who knows that the material body
Performs all kinds of deeds.
He sees that the self does nothing;
He is one who actually succeeds.

Knowledge brings spiritual peace
To a dedicated and faithful soul.
He is eligible for this achievement
When his senses are under control.

One whose doubts have been destroyed
By transcendental illumination
Is situated factually in the self,
Thus not bound by any reaction.

Surely, we get the fruits of our acts;
The Lord witnesses all of our actions.
We cannot hide anything from Him
For He pervades in all directions.

When irreligion is prominent in the family,
Women become polluted.
From this comes unwanted population
And purity becomes uprooted.

Unwanted population certainly causes hellish life
For the family and for those who destroy traditions.
They no longer give offerings of food and water
And their ancestors fall into deplorable conditions.

By the evil deeds of those
Who destroy the family tradition,
Birth of unwanted children increase
And family welfare activities end in ruination.

It is heard from the authorities–
And by the disciplic succession very well
That those who destroy family traditions
Will always dwell in hell.

Impurities are not befitting
A man who knows the value of life.
These do not lead to higher planets
But lead to infamy and strife.

The embodied soul passes in this body
From boyhood to youth to old age;
The soul passes into the next body at death;
A sober person is not bewildered at this stage.

One should not be disturbed by
The non-permanent heat and cold.
But knowing that they are temporary
One must be steady, tolerant and bold.

Spirit, which pervades the entire body.
Is indestructible, immeasurable and whole.
No one is able to destroy or slay
The ever-existing, imperishable soul.

As a person puts on new garments
Giving up the old ones he has worn,
The soul leaves his old body behind
And accepts a fresh one–newly born.

One who has taken his birth,
His death is definite and certain.
After the soul leaves the body
He is sure to take birth again.

Some look on the soul as amazing,
Some describe it in the same way.
Some while others, even after hearing,
Are perplexed and have nothing to say.

The soul who dwells in the body
Can never be slain.
So one need not grieve for any being
Nor feel any pain.

There is no birth and death
For the eternal, everlasting soul.
So lamentation for a temporary body
Never leads one to the supreme goal.

By neglecting one's own duty,
He loses his respectful reputation.
Dishonor is worse than death
For the honorable man's contemplation.

Those who are on the devotional path
Their purpose or aim is one.
Those who focus on many branches–
Their fruitful activities cannot be done.

Performing his prescribed duty
Unattached to the fruits of action,
Detached from success or failure,
He attains the state beyond all affliction.

A man engaged in devotional service
Rids himself of both good and bad reactions.
So one must strive for purifying yoga
Which is the art of all his actions.

Great sages stop such activities
That cause them to be born repeatedly.
They become free from the cycle of birth and death
And attain the state beyond all misery.

When one's intelligence has crossed
The dense forest of delusion,
Whatever he has heard or would hear
Will not cause him any confusion.

When one's mind is not disturbed
By the flowery Vedic word any more,
His mind becomes fixed in self-realized trance
And he attains divine consciousness for sure.

When one finds satisfaction within,
From giving up desires of mental concoction,
He attains pure transcendental consciousness
And is situated in his natural, pure position.

When one is not disturbed or elated
By the threefold miseries or contentment,
He is called a sage of steady mind
And is free from fear, anger and attachment.

One who is not affected by good or bad
Or any changes that he may meet,
Is fixed in perfect knowledge
Having attained the Lord's lotus feet.

A person free from all attachment and aversion
With controlled senses through regulation,
Engages his senses in the service of the Supreme
And obtains the Lord's complete compassion.

One who is satisfied in God consciousness–
His material miseries are diminished–
And in such satisfied consciousness,
One's intelligence is well established.

Without connection with the Supreme,
One has no intelligence or a steady mind.
Without this there's no possibility of peace;
There's no happiness without peace, one will find.

By engaging in service to the Lord,
One can gratify his senses.
It's the only way to curb material desires;
One then becomes a soul of steady intelligence.

Even just a few minutes before death,
Spiritual consciousness provides one freedom.
One gives up the process of material life
And enters into My eternal kingdom.

There are two classes of men
Who are trying for self-realization.
Some try through devotional service
And others through philosophical speculation.

Work done as a sacrifice for Vishnu
Frees one from material entanglement.
By performing duties for His satisfaction,
One no longer remains in material imprisonment.

The Lord provides all necessities
If one depends upon Him with belief.
To enjoy His gifts without reciprocation
One proves he is a thief.

Devotees first offer food to the Lord
And then become released from all sins.
Others who prepare food for sense pleasure
They eat nothing more than sin.

Sacrifice is born of prescribed duty;
This performance produces the rains.
The rains give to the land life subsistence
Feeding all living bodies by growing the grains.

Vedic scriptures come from the Supreme
And manifest His message and advice.
The Vedas prescribe regulated activities;
The Transcendence is situated in acts of sacrifice.

A human life without sacrifice
Achieves not any fruit or gain.
Living only for sense satisfaction
Such a person lives in vain.

He who takes pleasure in the self,
Whose life is for self-realization,
Is satisfied in the self only, fully satiated–
For him there is no duty or obligation.

A self-realized man has no purpose to fulfill
In the discharge of his prescribed duties.
Nor has he any reason not to perform such work
Nor needs to depend on other living entities.

One must perform his prescribed duty
Without attachment to the fruits of his action.
Being detached to success or to failure
One attains the Supreme for perfection.

Whatever action a great man performs
Common men follow in the same way.
Whatever standards he sets by example
All the world pursues without delay.

Being attached to the result of work,
Ignorant men work day and night.
Learned sages work without attachment
And lead people on the path that is right.

A learned sage should not stop
The work of those who desire reward.
He should engage and instruct them
To work in devotion for the Lord.

Due to false ego, the bewildered soul
Thinks he is the doer of all activities.
Actually, the three modes of material nature
Carry out all these different activities.

One who devotes himself to the Absolute Truth
Does not engage in sense enjoyment.
Knowing well the difference between the two actions:
Working in devotion or fruitive employment.

Faithful people do their duty
According to the Lord's injunctions.
They become free from all envy
And the bondage of fruitive actions.

Those who, out of envy, disregard My words
And follow their own direction,
Are bereft of all knowledge
And ruin their endeavors for perfection.

A Learned man acts according to his nature
Which is acquired from the three modes, too.
And everyone follows his nature,
So what can repression do?

There are stumbling blocks on the path
Such as attachment and aversion.
There are also regulative principles
To protect one from diversion.

To discharge one's own duty is better
Than engaging in another's duty.
For to follow another's path is dangerous
That does not bless inner peace and beauty.

It is all-devouring lust only
That forces one to impel for sinful act.
Later on, it transforms into wrath
Which is born with material contact.

The great symbol of sin (lust) can be curbed
By regulating the senses in the beginning of life.
This destroyer of knowledge and self-realization
Must be slain to end all one's strife.

Working senses are superior to dull matter,
The mind is higher than each sense.
Intelligence surpasses the mind
And the soul rules over the intelligence.

One should stabilize the restless mind
Through deliberate spiritual intelligence.
To conquer the foe of knowledge (lust)
One requires the strength of spiritual excellence.

Being freed from attachment, fear and anger
And taking complete refuge in Me,
Many sages have purified themselves
And they all attained pure love for Me.

Any person who searches for Me,
I reward him according to his surrender.
Everyone, in all respects, follows My path
And gets results according to the activities he renders.

There is no work that affects Me,
Nor do I aspire for the fruits of action.
Knowing this truth about Me,
One becomes free from fruitive reactions.

Understanding the Supreme Lord's nature
Liberated souls acted long ago.
By firmly following in their footsteps,
We should perform our duties and spiritually grow.

One who is always satisfied with gain
Which comes of its own accord;
He's steady, non-envious, free from duality
And ready to satisfy the Lord.

One who works unattached to material nature.
And is fully situated in divine intelligence.
Such a person is free from all dualities
And becomes situated in full transcendence.

Fully absorbed in spiritual activities
Takes one to the Lord's eternal place.
And when he does everything for the Absolute,
He can then see Him face-to-face.

Full contribution to spiritual activities
Brings one to the Lord's eternal abode.
Then consummation is offered to the Absolute
The contributor gets the same spiritual mode.

Some engage their hearing and senses
Carefully through mental control.
Others restrict their senses
To attain a higher goal.

One who wants to achieve self-realization,
By controlling the senses and the mind,
Offers the functions of all the senses and breath
As oblations into the fire of the steady mind.

Some with strict vows become enlightened
By sacrificing their possessions.
They perform austerities in yoga, study the Vedas
And become elevated in their perception.

Those who know the meaning of sacrifice,
Have success for past sinful reaction to clear.
Having tasted the nectarous result of such work,
They advance toward the supreme atmosphere.

There's no happiness on this planet
In this life or in the next event.
Without performing sacrifice
How can one be content?

One can know different sacrifices
From the Vedas and attain liberation.
That sacrifice performed in knowledge
Is better than sacrificing material possessions.

Real knowledge from a self-realized soul
Saves one from falling into illusion.
He then sees all beings as My parts,
And they are Mine: This is My conclusion.

Knowledge brings spiritual peace
To a dedicated and faithful soul.
He is eligible for this achievement
When his senses are under control.

Ignorant and faithless persons
Who doubt the sacred text.
Won't experience God consciousness
In this world or in the next.

One whose doubts have been destroyed
By transcendental illumination
Is situated factually in the self,
Thus not bound by any reaction.

Doubts should be slashed by the weapon of wisdom
And from ignorance these doubts arise.
With yoga one can fight these doubts
And then see with spiritual eyes.

The renunciation of work or work in devotion;
Both paths are good for liberation.
But, of the two, work for the Supreme
Surpasses the path of renunciation.

One who neither hates nor desires
The fruits of his action and endeavor
He is free from all dualities
And gets liberation from bondage forever.

Detachment from matter and attachment for the Lord;
Both processes are one and the same.
People who see things as they are –
Their life has a spiritual aim.

A thoughtful person in devotional service
Achieves the Supreme without delay.
Others miss this opportunity
By renouncing all activities and play.

Pure souls work in devotion
By controlling their senses and mind.
They love everyone and everyone loves them
Though always working, their works never bind.

One who performs his duty
Offering all results to the Supreme,
Is unaffected by sinful actions
As a lotus untouched by a stream.

Using body, mind, intelligence and senses
Yogis act without material contamination.
Abandoning attachment, they do their duty
Only for the purpose of purification.

Without union with the Divine
One's entangled in fruits of one's work forever.
The steadily devoted soul gets peace
By offering the result of his endeavor.

When one is enlightened with knowledge,
Nescience is destroyed and goes away.
Knowledge reveals everything to him
As sun lights up the day.

When one's intelligence, mind, faith and refuge
All are fixed in the Godly theme,
One becomes fully cleansed of misgivings
And proceeds on the path to the Supreme.

Those who have equal vision
Treat all living beings as friends.
They see the Supersoul in everyone's heart
And their understanding never bends.

Winning birth and death, having equanimity of mind
All are signs of self-realization.
Those who reach this stage are flawless
And are eligible to attain the highest elevation.

A liberated person neither rejoices nor laments
And knows the science of the soul.
He's intelligent and not bewildered
Understanding what is life's goal.

One who's liberated is not attracted to sense pleasure
But enjoys the pleasure within in extreme.
Unlimited happiness illuminates his way
For he concentrates on the Supreme.

A wise man does not delight in sense pleasure
That is of short duration and a source of misery.
A liberated soul is not interested in anything
That is not permanent but temporary.

Sages don't relish sensual pleasures
That have a beginning and an end.
They enjoy their eternal happiness
Serving their dear, Supreme Friend.

Before giving up this present body,
If one is able to check anger and desire,
He is well situated and happy in this world
Tolerating the urges of material fire.

One who is active and rejoices within,
Whose aim is inward, is a perfect mystic.
He is liberated in the Supreme and attains Him
Not being interested in anything materialistic.

Those free from anger and material desires,
Who are self-realized and self-controlled;
They constantly endeavor for perfection –
They become liberated and reach their goal.

One who's in full consciousness of the Lord
Knows He's the beneficiary of all austerities.
Knowing the Supreme is the well-wisher of all,
He attains peace from the material miseries.

A sage is one who performs his duty
Not one who lights no fire.
Action is better than renunciation
And an honest soul works without desire.

Controller of the mind meets God
Attaining eternal tranquility;
Accepting joy, pain, heat and cold
With patience and equanimity.

A person is considered even more advanced
When he regards all with equal eyes:
Well-wishers, enemies, friends,
Sinners, pious. envious and wise.

With an unaggressive mind, devoid of fear,
Completely free from intimate relation;
One should think of Me within his heart
And make Me life's ultimate destination.

Controlling the body, mind and activities
Through endeavoring and persistence,
One attains the kingdom of God
Through cessation of material existence.

When the mind is perfectly disciplined,
One becomes situated in transcendence.
He controls all his material desires
And properly uses his independence.

One who never deviates from the path
And who is fixed in yoga with faith and determination
one should abandon, without exception
All material desires born of mental speculation.

The yogi whose mind is fixed on God
Attains transcendental happiness in extreme.
Being free from his former sins,
He realizes his identity with the Supreme.

A devotee is a perfect yogi
Aware of everyone's happiness and distress.
He has equal vision and all care
And he helps others spiritually progress.

It is not an easy process to curb
The turbulent, obstinate, restless mind.
But by suitable practice and detachment
It is possible, the way to find.

For one whose mind is unbridled,
Self-realization is not easy to attain.
But success shines over one's path
If the mind is controlled and is sane.

A yogi reaches a greater stage
Than the empiricist, fruitive worker and ascetic.
The Lord instructs one to be a yogi in all situations
To attain spiritual knowledge which is ecstatic.

Of all yogis who think of Me
And always with faith abide in Me,
Who render loving service to Me–
They are the most intimately united with Me.

By practicing yoga in consciousness of Me
You will be freed from your doubtful mind.
Being attached to Me in complete thoughts,
The ultimate knowledge you will find.

The knowledge of the phenomenal world
And numinous world I shall explain.
After having this deep wisdom,
Nothing further to know remains.

Out of many thousands among men,
One may endeavor for perfection.
Hardly one knows Me in truth
Unless he follows My direction.

No truth is superior to Me,
The Lord has clearly said.
Everything rests upon Me
As pearls are strung on a thread.

The whole world is deluded
By goodness, passion and ignorance.
The Lord is inexhaustible and the highest;
Still, the world does not know His presence.

The three modes of material nature
Are difficult to overcome.
But those who have surrendered to Me
Easily cross them and blissful they become.

When illusion steals one's knowledge,
One becomes foolish and unable to see.
He partakes of the demonic, atheistic nature
And does not surrender unto Me.

Four kinds of souls take to God's shelter
Distressed, inquisitive, desirer of fruit [wealth];
Among all pious men the best is he
Who is searching for knowledge of the Absolute.

I consider to be just like My own self
He who is situated in knowledge of Me.
Being engaged in My transcendental service,
Such a soul is sure to attain Me.

I am dear to him and he is dear to Me–
One with knowledge is divine and blessed.
He who is engaged in My service–
Among all living beings, he is the best.

After many births and deaths
One who has knowledge and has care,
Surrenders unto Me as the cause of all;
To find such a great soul is rare.

Those whose spiritual sense is stolen by desires
Surrender to the demigods for material achievement.
They worship according to their own natures
For their own immediate fulfillment.

I sit in one's heart as Supersoul
And help him steadily fix his devotion
To the demigod he wants to worship,
But he remains in the material ocean.

One who worships a demigod
Eventually has his desires fulfilled.
But he doesn't know that these benefits
Are ones that I have willed.

All results bestowed by demigods
Are limited and temporary.
Those who worship demigods go to them
But My devotees are with Me eternally.

When one has small intelligence,
He understands My eternal form as unknowable.
He does not know My higher nature
Which is supreme and imperishable.

The Lord never manifests Himself
To the foolish and unintelligent entity.
He is covered by His internal potency
That He's the unborn and infallible personality.

I know all that happened in the past
And know what is going to be.
I am also aware of the present situation;
I know all beings, but no one knows Me.

All living entities are born into delusion
And into dualities, they shall remain.
Bewildered by desire and hate,
The higher taste, they cannot gain.

Souls who have done pious activities
In this life time and in the past;
They serve Me with determination;
Their delusions no longer last.

One who knows about transcendental activities,
He is actually intelligent and is wise.
He takes shelter in Me through devotional service;
And gains liberation from old age and demise.

Knowing that I rule the material manifestation
And the demigods and methods of sacrifice;
One can understand Me as the Supreme
Even at the critical time of demise.

The spirit soul is part of the Supreme
And his natural propensity is to serve.
If he forgets his real identity and position,
He gets different bodies as he deserves.

Whatever state of mind one has
When the time of death prevails,
He will proceed to that same state
In his next life, without fail.

He who meditates on Me, the Supreme Lord,
Carrying out all his prescribed engagements,
With all his activities dedicated to Me,
I bring him to My abode making all arrangements.

Great souls in their devotion
Return not to this world of pain.
Achieving the ultimate goal of life;
No higher perfection to attain.

This world is temporary and full of miseries;
It is declared by the Supreme Personality.
By engaging in His loving devotional service,
We can go to His abode of bliss and eternity.

From the highest to the lowest planet
Wherein birth and death take place;
One who attains the supreme abode
Won't take birth again in any case.

The material nature manifests
And unmanifests again and again.
Yet there is another nature
That is supreme and always remains.

Sages describe the unmanifest and infallible
Which is known as the supreme destination.
Having attained My supreme abode
One never returns to the land of lamentation.

The all-pervading Lord is present everywhere,
Both in the material and spiritual ocean.
His position is greater than the greatest
And He is attained by unalloyed devotion.

Devotees know there are two paths
To pass from this worldly ocean:
One in light and one in darkness –
They're not disturbed being fixed in devotion.

Engaging in devotional service provides all benefits
Of performing sacrifices and giving in charity.
Gaining the results of philosophical and fruitive activities
And finally reaches the Supreme Personality.

If one knows that the soul is different than the body,
That the soul's eternal and can't be destroyed;
He knows this confidential part of knowledge:
This material world can't be enjoyed.

This transcendental knowledge
Is the king of education.
And it is the purest knowledge
Giving direct perception of the self by realization.

As the mighty wind blows everywhere
Yet always rests in the sky,
All created beings are everywhere
And in Me they rest and rely.

One who does sacrifice with knowledge
Worships the Lord in His personal form.
The Supreme as the one without a second
As diverse in many and in the universal form.

Once one's pious credits run out,
He returns to this mortal earth.
If he seeks more enjoyment through the Vedas,
He will again cycle through death and birth.

Those who faithfully worship other demigods
Actually worship Me alone.
But they do so in a wrong way
Because they do it on their own.

I am the only enjoyer and master
Of every sacrifice.
Those not recognizing My true nature
Fall down being less wise.

Those who worship the demigods
Or forefathers, ghosts and spirits shall be
Born among such beings
But My worshipers will live with Me.

Whatever we eat, give, austerities perform,
Should be done as offerings to the Lord;
That frees us from good and bad results,
Bringing us to Him, the highest reward.

Pure love and devotion is important
Not opulent offering or treasure;
Even a leaf, flower, fruit or water
The Lord accepts with great pleasure.

Work performed as a sacrifice
For the Lord's satisfaction;
No bondage of work remains
And one is freed from all reaction.

Being freed from good and bad results
And fixing your mind on the Lord,
You will clear the mirror of your mind
And attain His planet, the highest award.

I envy no one, nor am partial to anyone;
Equality to all is My natural trend.
But one who renders devotional service to Me
Is Mine and I am his dearest friend.

The power of devotional service purifies
Even one who's committed abominable action.
He should be considered a saintly person
As properly situated in his determination.

The Lord's devotee never perishes
But lives forever with all dignity.
As the devotional service imparts
All bliss, knowledge and eternity.

In devotional service it does not matter;
There is no discrimination.
Even if one is of a lower birth
He is eligible for the supreme destination.

It is not habitable for a sane gentleman –
This temporary world full of pains and wrath.
No one should remain here forever to suffer
But come to Me by following the devotional path.

Be My devotee, think of Me,
Bow down and worship Me;
Being fully absorbed in Me
You will certainly come to Me.

You know Yourself by Your internal potency
O, Supreme Person, origin of all,
Lord of all beings and of the universe –
You are the worshipful Lord of all.

Neither demigods nor great sages
Know My original, opulent mystery.
Though, in every respect, I am the source
Of all demigods and sages that be.

He who knows Me as unborn and beginningless,
As the Supreme Lord of all the worlds that be,
He is the only undeluded among all beings
And from all sins, he becomes free.

I create these various qualities of all:
Intelligence, forgiveness, austerity,
Happiness, distress, fame, infamy,
Knowledge, satisfaction and equanimity.

One who is factually convinced
Of My opulence and power without doubt,
He links with Me in devotional service
Always firm, steady and devout.

Everything emanates from Me:
All spiritual and material parts.
Learned sages know this well
And worship Me with all their hearts.

All great sages confirm this truth:
You are the ultimate abode and purest,
The eternal, transcendental, original person,
The Supreme Personality, unborn and the greatest.

The unlimited, mystic power of Your opulences
You alone can fathom, not anyone else in this world.
I am never satiated, for the more I hear
The more I want to taste the nectar of Your words.

You are the resting place of all this universe,
The inexhaustible, supreme, primal objective.
You are the maintainer of the eternal religion,
The Personality of Godhead and most attractive.

Your holy name brings joy to the whole world;
All become attached to You, o, master of the senses.
The demons are afraid, running here and there
But the sages pay their humble obeisances.

O limitless one, God of gods, refuge of the world,
You are the original one, the greatest of the great,
You are the invincible source, the cause of all causes;
You transcend this universe that You alone create.

You are the supreme refuge, above the modes,
The original, oldest, You know all that is known.
The ultimate sanctuary of the whole cosmic world
And this manifestation is pervaded by You alone.

You are the supreme controller,
Brahma, air, water, moon and fire.
To offer my obeisances a thousand times
Unto You is my deep desire.

I bow down from the front and back
And unto You from the left and right.
You are the all-pervading Supreme Personality
And the master of limitless might.

Not knowing Your glories, I have done wrongs
In madness, love or relaxation.
O infallible, kindly excuse my offenses
That I've foolishly made in friendly conversation.

You are the father of the cosmic manifestation,
The spiritual master and worshipable chief.
No one is equal to or greater than You –
Your shelter relieves us from material grief.

As a friend tolerates impertinence of a friend
As a father tolerates impudence of his son
Or a wife tolerates the familiarity of her husband –
Kindly tolerate all the wrongs I may have done.

Only by undivided service to Me
Can I be understood and be seen.
This is right way to enter My mysteries;
No other process has there been.

One engaged in devotional service,
Friendly to all and in thoughts of Me,
Free from mental speculation and fruitive activities
Making Me the goal, surely comes to Me.

Whoever's mind is fixed on My personal form
And is always engaged in worshiping My feet,
Such faithful and devoted souls
I consider the most perfect and complete.

Whoever is attached to the Lord's impersonal feature,
Advancement is very troublesome for him.
Therefore, on the path of formless meditation,
Progress is always difficult and dim.

For those who worship and serve Me
Meditating and fixing their minds,
I quickly deliver them from birth and death,
From bodies of all kinds.

One who is a kind friend to all
And always acts without false pride;
Tolerant in peace or in disturbance
Such a soul is self-satisfied.

This body is the field and one who
Knows this is the knower of the field.
He knows this body undergoes many changes
And only short-term happiness can he yield.

To understand this material body
And the eternal soul in which it runs
Is the science of knowledge
And the Supersoul knows the field of everyone.

The knowledge and knower of activities
Is described by those who are wise.
The explanation's in the Vedanta-sutra
As to the cause and effect of our lives.

By knowing the spirit soul,
One can taste life's nectar.
Knowing he's beginningless and subordinate to Me,
He sees Me as his protector.

The material nature and the living entities
Are the energy of the Lord.
They are beginningless and their transformations
Are products that material nature awards.

One changes his body as one changes his dress
Due to his association with the material variety.
One meets good and evil among various species
Due to his desire to lord it over material society.

The Supersoul exists in our hearts
As the permitter, witness and seer.
He allows us the freedom to follow
The path of distress or of cheer.

By clear understanding of the material nature,
The Supersoul, individual soul and their interrelation,
One can finish the cycle of birth and death
And can attain everlasting liberation.

Some begin to worship the Lord
After hearing from authorities.
Because of their tendency to hear
They transcend birth and death calamities.

One who knows that the material body
Performs all kinds of deeds
And sees that the self does nothing;
He is one who actually sees.

When one stops seeing the different identities
Due to different bodies of the soul,
He sees how beings are expanded everywhere
And attains the transcendental goal.

One with the vision of eternity can see
The imperishable soul beyond nature's modes.
The soul neither does anything nor is entangled
Despite activities in contact with the bodily abodes.

The sky, due to its subtle nature,
Is all-pervading but doesn't mix with anything.
Similarly, the soul situated in Brahman
Is in the body but is aloof from everything.

As the sun is situated in one place
But is illuminating the universe
The material body is illuminated
By the consciousness of the spirit soul.

Those who see with eyes of knowledge
Distinguish between the body and soul.
They understand the process of liberation
And attain the supreme goal.

One in knowledge can attain My nature
Having attained the highest perfection.
Thus one is not born at the time of creation
Or disturbed at the time of dissolution.

All species are made possible by birth
When I, the original Father, plant the seed.
The combination of material and spiritual nature
Is required for all of this to proceed.

Material nature consists of three modes:
Goodness, passion and ignorance.
The living entity becomes conditioned by these
When he comes in contact with their existence.

Goodness conditions one to happiness,
Passion to fruitive action.
Ignorance covers one's knowledge
And binds one to madness and distraction.

When men see the modes controlling
All the activities that they do,
They can know the Supreme Lord
And attain the spiritual realm, too.

When one transcends nature's three modes,
He can enjoy nectarous happiness.
He becomes free from birth, death and old age
And their ultimate, intense distress.

One who engages in devotional service,
Unfailing in any kind of situation,
Transcends the modes of material nature
And thus comes to the level of perfection.

One who is not bewildered, done with material lust,
Free from false prestige, illusion and association,
Knows how to surrender unto Me
And attains the highest destination.

My abode requires no illumination
From the sun, moon, fire or electricity.
Going there, one never comes back
To this world full of pains and complexity.

Conditioned souls, My fragmental parts,
Want freedom which is hard to find.
They struggle hard with their six senses
Which also include the mind.

In the temporary material world
Every living entity is fallible.
In the eternal spiritual world
Every living entity is infallible.

Besides the fallible and infallible living entities,
There is the greatest person, the Supersoul.
The imperishable Lord Himself
Enters and maintains the worlds of all.

As I am transcendental beyond both
The conditioned and liberated entities,
I am the greatest and celebrated in this world;
The Vedas praise Me as the Supreme Personality.

Whoever knows Me as the Supreme Person,
Putting all his doubts away;
He is the knower of everything
And serves Me with devotion every day.

He who discards scriptural injunctions
And acts according to his own whim,
Attains not the supreme destination;
Happiness and perfection are dim.

The transcendental divine qualities
Are conducive to liberation.
But the demoniac qualities keep one
In bondage to this material creation.

One who gives up lust, anger and greed
And performs acts for self-realization,
Step-by-step he gradually attains
The highest and supreme destination.

He who discards scriptural injunctions
And acts according to his own whim,
Attains not the supreme destination;
Happiness and perfection are dim.

By learning what is duty and what is not
By the Veda's rules and regulations,
By acting according to their teachings,
One may gradually reach the highest elevation.

Foolish persons perform austerity and penance
Disregarding scriptures out of ego and pride.
Such deluded souls are no more than demons
Who torture their body and the Supersoul inside.

Sages undertaking performances
Of sacrifice, penance and charity
Begin with om as taught in the scriptures
And can attain the Supreme Personality.

Anything done without transcendental objectives,
Whether it be sacrifice, penance or charity,
Is useless both in this life and the next
If one has no faith in the Supreme Personality.

The renounced order of life means
To give up material activities based on greed.
The wise men say renunciation means
To give up the result of each deed.

One should not renounce purifying acts
Of sacrifice, penance and charity.
Even great souls perform such activities
To build and maintain their purity.

Sacrifices should be done as a duty:
This is the final opinion of the Supreme Absolute.
These activities should be accepted by one
Without attachment or any expectation of fruit.

Anyone who renounces his duties
Out of fear and bodily discomforts;
His renunciation never leads to the goal
As there's no elevation in passionate efforts.

The intelligent renouncer in goodness
Neither hates nor hankers for any acts.
He does his duty at the proper time and place
Without fearing any troublesome effects.

One who is beyond all doubts and fears
And is situated in the mode of goodness,
Does his work as a duty
And achieves everlasting happiness.

One accrues after one's death
Actions that are desirable, undesirable and mixed.
But for one who is renounced has no such results
And his God conscious destination is fixed.

Worshiping the Supreme, the source of all beings
Who is pervading in all the directions;
Through performing his own work
A man can surely get perfection.

Devotees don't think themselves proprietors.
They are free from false ego and pride;
Whether time is favorable or not,
They are tolerant and satisfied.

Depend upon Me in all activities,
Work always under My protection.
In such pure devotional service,
Be conscious of Me and attain perfection.

If one becomes conscious of the Lord,
He will clear all obstacles away.
But acting through his false ego,
He will be lost and will not find his way.

The Lord directs everyone's wanderings
And is situated in their hearts.
These entities are seated as on a machine
Which is made of material parts.

Material nature fashions a certain body
To a certain type of living entity.
He has to work under that bodily situation
Under the control of the Supreme Personality.

Just surrender unto Me utterly;
My grace will flow through.
You will attain transcendental peace
And My supreme and eternal abode, too.

Once one surrenders to the Supreme,
Automatically anxieties stay away.
He kindly and completely takes charge
Illuminating each blissful day.

I speak this most confidential knowledge
To you, My friend, as My supreme instruction.
Just surrender unto Me and you will come to Me;
This is life's highest perfection.

As promised by the Lord Supreme:
Think of Me, become My devotee.
Then you will return to Me without fail
By worshiping and offering homage to Me.

Simply surrender unto the Lord;
Be delivered from all sinful reaction.
The Supreme Savior of all living entities
Gives surrendered souls all protection.

One who spreads the Lord's message
Is the Supersoul's most dear.
He will go back to the eternal abode
The Lord's guarantee is sure and clear.

Wherever there is the Supreme Lord
And wherever pure devotees reside,
Opulence, victory, power and morality
Miraculously arise from each side.

The Author

Krishna Priya Dasi was born in India in 1972 with several severe physical challenges. Standing less than four feet tall, she encountered major structural and bone problems. As a child, her physical condition prevented her from getting a traditional academic education; however, her interest and love for art, poetry and spirituality was deeply ingrained from the beginning of her life. She kept herself engaged with her activities, but, as an adult, another heavy challenge awaited her.

Forced to undergo major brain surgery in 2005, she almost died, but miraculously stayed in this physical body for some larger purpose. She decided to write this book inspired by the teachings of *Bhagavada-gita As It Is* written by His Divine Grace A.C. Bhaktivedanta Swami Prabhupada. She also did the simple hand paintings of lotuses despite health challenges of eye/hand coordination and extreme dizziness. She now dedicates this to all special souls who love the Supreme Creator and His created living beings and who may also face daunting and intense physical obstacles.

She also builds and maintains her own website,
www.supersoul.com/Krishna
or email: krsnapriyad@hotmail.com

Her books and her art works can be purchased at her website.